SUMMER SOLSTICE
CELEBRATION

How to Organize Your Own Event

Estelle Reder

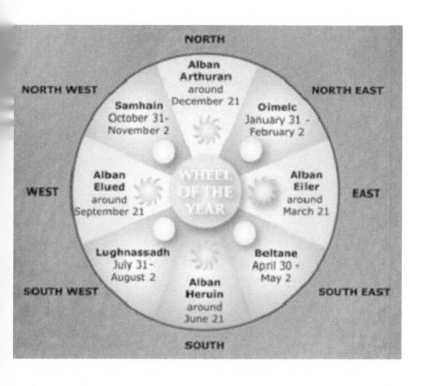

HOW TO CELEBRATE THE SUMMER SOLSTICE

One of the four Celtic Festivals is called Alban Heruin – summer solstice: the light of the shore. It is also referred to as Litha or Midsummer's Day.

Two of the fire festivals, Samhain and Beltane, were considered to be male, and Imbolc and Lughnasadh were female. Each Festival was celebrated for three days – before, during and after the official day of observance.

It was traditionally celebrated out in the forest with picnics, games, and a large bonfire. – for three days from sunset around 21 June according to the Astronomical calendar, for power, joy and courage.

This book is focused only on the summer solstice celebration and how you can organize your own event.

CONTENTS

INTRODUCTION

Beltane joyfully heralded the arrival of Summer in its full glory. It was believed that if you bathed in the dew of a Beltane morning, your beauty would flourish throughout the year. On the eve of Beltane, the Celts would build two large fires, created from the nine sacred woods, in honour of Summer. The tribal herds were ritually driven between them, so as to purify and protect them in the upcoming year.

The fires celebrate the return of life and fruitfulness to the earth. The Celebration includes frolicking throughout the countryside, dancing the Maypole, leaping over fires, and "going a'maying".

It was customary for young lovers to spend the night in the forest. Beltane is the time of sensuality revitalized, the reawakening of the earth and all of her children. It is the time when tribal people celebrate with joy the vivid colours and vibrant scents of the season, tingling summer breezes, and the rapture of summer after a long dormant winter.

It is customary that Handfastings take place at this time. A handfasting was originally more like an engagement period, where two people would declare a binding union between themselves for a year and a day.

The original handfasting was a trial marriage. It gave the couple the chance to see if they could survive marriage to each other.

After a year goes by (a handfasting was once believed to last a year and a day), the couple could either split as if they had never been married or could decide to enter permanently into marriage.

This custom is becoming popular again.

Another custom was to leap over the Beltane bonfire. Young people jumped the fire for luck in finding a spouse, travelers jumped the fire to ensure a safe journey, and pregnant women jumped the fire to assure an easy delivery.

PART I: BACKGROUND

The Summer Solstice Ritual is an extremely powerful ritual that lays the foundation of the summer. The purpose of this ritual is to renew, release and enhance our external physical manifestations - financial, health, joy, faith, love, happiness, friendships, family, blessings

For couples: it is also a time for renewing the bonds of love that brought the two of you together in the first place. Remember that song from the 1978 movie "Grease" with Olivia Newton-John and John Travolta called "Summer Nights" ... the amazing feelings of youthful passionate love ... bu-ut, oh! Those su-ummer nights .... With renewed energy of the Summer Solstice - all things are possible.

The time of full outward physical manifestation is here. The powers of inner contemplation are at their lowest point, and everywhere are the energies of "doing," of exerting the will.

In ancient times it was considered a time of fullness of life, worldly blessings and celebration. Not much has changed today in how we look at summer.

We see it as a time of vacations, play, celebration, fun, joviality, parties, and barbecues with family and friends at the beach or park. Days are longer which gives us more time to enjoy the sun and soak in its warmth.

The Summer Solstice celebrates the joy, warmth and laughter of summer; and God's power. The Solstice is a day to see the Creator in everyone you come in contact with and to recognize their divinity along with the recognition of your own self God image.

As we experience the warm, full power of the Solstice Sun, we are called to make true on earth the words of the Master Jesus, "I and the Father are One." To understand this is to recognize the divinity in everyone we meet. Use this day to see God in each person you meet.

Celebrating the Summer Solstice

I n ceremony, we bring together eternal timelessness and temporal time. Through ceremony we connect the eternal rhythms with daily living.

We allow our world to be illuminated by the grander world of the cosmos, of the seasons, of the rites of passage universal to all beings –birthing, growing, maturing, dying, and rebirthing.

Ceremonies reflect our knowing: We are related to the eternal source from which all life flows and returns. By doing ceremony together, we become the ceremony. Doing ceremony together, we learn to live in a Sacred Way. At the very heart of shamanic living dwells the understanding of the profound significance of doing ceremonies.

And now comes around the turning time called the Summer Solstice and here we offer some examples of what Circles might do to celebrate this seasonal shifting of the Wheel of Life.

Chapter 1: Planning Your Event

The Summer Solstice is the longest day and the shortest night of the year. Following this Solstice, the days get shorter, and the nights longer. The dark slowly begins to take over the cycle until we arrive at the time of Winter Solstice.

In some cultures, Summer Solstice is also known as "Midsummer's Night" and the ceremonies begin with twilight. For others, the ceremony begins with Sunrise, continues through the day and the night.

In the Far North, the Sun shines continuously--a blessing for those who endured the long, long months of darkness. Celebrations may continue for several days. At Summer Solstice, the Sun and Earth align in such a way as to assist all growing things to come into their fullness.

Thus, the Summer Solstice ceremonies are often full of dancing, singing, dressing up in costumes and holding theatrical performances, feasting.

It is a time when Earth and all her inhabitants join in mutual celebration and ecstasy. A time of rejoicing for the blessings bestowed from the marriage of Heaven and Earth.

Chapter 2: Planning Information

Animal: Bear
Tree: Oak
Herbs and incenses:
chamomile
elder
fennel
lavender,
St. John's Wort
verbena

Candle colours:
red, orange, gold

Crystals:
brilliant red
orange crystals

Stones of the sun:
Amber
carnelian
orange
beryl
jasper
crystal quartz.

Agricultural significance: The long days and warm weather are vital for long hours in the fields as young animals grow strong and crops begin to ripen; but there is an awareness that the Summer Solstice does mark the longest day of the year and that henceforth, though imperceptibly darkness increases; this is a reminder that time is finite and chores cannot be put off indefinitely.

Folk/magical significance: The Sun God is crowned by the Goddess and for this one day takes his place as her equal. But it is joy tinged with sadness for the Dark Twin is born and grows stronger, even as the Sun King becomes weaker, day by day. The Goddess or her priestess/Druidess representative, casts her bouquet on a hilltop fire to add her power to the sun and to pay tribute to him.

As at the Midwinter Solstice, strength is given to the sun. Fire wheels were rolled from the tops of hills and flaming tar barrels and torches hurled into the air. In the Sun Goddess tradition, she was said to bathe in the waters of the earth on the Solstice Eve and so river water was (before pollution) regarded as especially healing for bathing at dawn on Summer Solstice morn.

Ritual significance: The day of pure *Awen* (loosely translated from Welsh, it means flowing spirit, or flowing inspiration. ... In any case, drinking from the cauldron of the Goddess is to drink deeply of *Awen*) as the three bars of Light appear at Dawn.

Awen is chanted out loud or intoned silently within the soul and is made up of three sounds: Ah-oo-en. The Ah sound opens you to life, evokes joy and purpose, radiates power and creativity. The oo sound expands, continues, and disseminates the energy and power you have opened to, allowing it to blossom. The enn sound completes the process, creates the boundary, the containment, and both grounds and gives birth to all that the previous two sounds have inspired and generated.

Alban Heruin (Celtic for Summer Solstice) was the longest day of the year.

Stonehenge is oriented to mark the sunrise at the summer and winter solstices. Druidic ceremonies are held at Dawn and Noon on the Solstice at sacred circles and stones and some groups and individuals keep a vigil from sunset on the previous evening.

At sunset of the Summer Solstice, another significant ritual points the Heel (Sun) Stone outside the circles at Stonehenge which casts a shadow on the Altar Stone, thus marking the beginning of the dying of the year.

Deities: *Sulis* (Minerva). At the sacred Celtic hot springs at Baths, the Romans built their own magnificent healing edifices, combining the indigenous *Sulis*, the Celtic Sun Goddess and resident patroness of the sacred waters at Bath, with their own Minerva Goddess of Wisdom.

Symbols: Use brightly-coloured flowers, oak boughs, golden fern pollen that is said to reveal buried treasure wherever it falls, scarlet, orange and yellow ribbons, gold coloured coins, sun-catchers and golden fruit.

Summer Solstice rituals are good for success, happiness, strength, identity, wealth, fertility, adolescents and young adults, career and travel.

Chapter 3: Personal Activities

On your own, you could greet the dawn by lighting a lantern just before sunrise, from an East facing hill or plain.

Honour the sun's most glorious day. It will spark your sense of wonder. Spend the day in the open air and then say farewell to the Sun on a West facing slope, lighting your lantern once more to give the sun power even as it descends.

You could cast golden flowers or herbs into the air from a hill, a handful at a time, making empowering statements for courage and achievement. Where they land and take root represents in   the old traditions' places of buried treasure or in this case symbolizes new or buried talents you can develop to realize your hidden potential.

Have a drink to the sun., Enjoy a cup of ginger and/or cinnamon tea in a scooped-out apple and orange with the sun- a cup for you and one for the sun, and offer a toast of admiration and thanksgiving, possibly working in a request that he provide you with a potent dose of his radiant power and confidence.

Set an intention that feels right. Considering the dual energies of expansion and release at work during the solstice (especially a full moon solstice!) work in an opening to that which you desire (love and connection), as well as a release or surrender of all that stands in the way of that desire.

Consider the mechanism of opening up to the full brightness of the moment while also allowing yourself to let go of any old stuff that no longer serves. To do this, consider incorporating their phrases "surrender to," "open up to," or "allow."

You could make your Solstice water, the most potent Sun water of the year, leaving water in a gold coloured dish surrounded by golden-coloured flowers from dusk on the Solstice Eve until Noon on the Longest Day. This is especially healing and empowering and you can keep it in clear glass or gold coloured bottles to drink or add to bath water to give you energy and confidence.

On the Water theme, if you have little ones take them to the beach, lake or river! Or simply give them a bucket of water and let them have some WATER PLAY! It's summer after all!

Have a dunk in a moving body of water. Summer Solstice is a time of both solar and lunar energies, as it's the time when the sun moves into the lunar, watery sign of Cancer. So even if you just stand ankle-deep in a stream, place yourself in a fresh, moving body of water and let it cleanse, invigorate, and rejuvenate your soul.

MANDALA

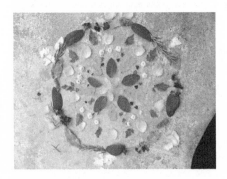

Make a small mandala with flowering herbs of Midsummer vervain and St John's Wort, sun herbs such as frankincense, juniper, rosemary and saffron and rose petals or all yellow or golden flowers. Arrange them in the form of a wheel and fill in the centre with tiny golden crystals or glass nuggets. You can breathe in the golden light from your living sun wheel.

OR … make a **SUN WHEEL** by creating a large wreath with flowers and moss. Then get some strips of paper and have your friends write a wish on it and wrap it or tie it with string to the wreath. Pass it around casually through the evening. Some can take turns dancing with it, holding it and then at the end of the evening throw it into a fire!

OR … celebrate with a summer **BONFIRE**! Play drums, dance and celebrate with your loved ones. Gather some fresh herbs like Vervain, Lavender, St. John's Wort or whatever is local. Throw them into the fire with your deepest wishes!

For a super fun idea make or buy a **SUN PINATA** and fill it with yellow flower petals and gold coins! Blindfold guests to hit it! **Note:** *There are great sites that give you step-by-step instructions on how to make your own sun piñata.*

SOLSTICE FLOWER ESSENCE
Make your own flower essences. They are so easy and magical to make!

Go out and tune in to the flower you are resonating with! Pick one flower and make one essence at a time. Use your intuition to feel whether or not you have permission to pick the flower(s). You can look up the energy that certain flowers carry; but do this only after you choose your flower – trust your own instincts!

Place your flower(s) in a small glass bowl with Spring water. Let it sit in direct sunlight for 3-4 hours, enough for the sun's rays into help the energy of the flower expand vibrationally into the water.

Strain the flowers with filter paper or strainer and pour into a bottle or jar.

Half fill your jar with your water and then add the same amount (fill the other half) with Brandy to preserve it. The essence you have left over, you can either drink or return it to the Earth as an offering of gratitude!

Then cap your jar, label the flower and date and you have your "MOTHER" essence! You can get a little dropper bottle and fill 1/4 way with Brandy and then simply add 2 or 3 drops of your "MOTHER" essence into your dropper bottle.

Since it's vibrational medicine a few drops are all it takes to carry the energy signature of the flower. This "dropper" bottle is what you can then use by adding a few drops into your water to sip through the day! Voila! you can have your "Solstice Flower Essence."

Note: Be conscious of how your body feels after you start using it. They are very gentle and safe to use but they move things energetically so pay attention – use your intuition and your discretion!

Altar of Light and Gratitude

For a more personal celebration, make a little altar of light and gratitude by lighting a candle (or few) and decorating it with summer flowers, and tangerines.

If you leave the tangerines outside in the sun, they will soak up the sun's energy and you can eat them later.

Also, you can stick a candle into an orange and make a beautiful candle holder.

Free your spirit

You can do this ritual by yourself or with your partner, friend(s) or family. This Solstice, the time is right to honestly assess the beliefs and habits that have been weighing you down or holding you back.

For example, have you been keeping yourself small out of the belief that it will make others more comfortable, or out of the fear that being yourself will scare people off? Or have you been telling negative stories about yourself that limit your truly fabulous nature? Or maybe you've been pursuing a goal or attempting to perpetuate a status quo that just isn't nourishing your soul?

As you observe the awesome power of the sun this Solstice, shine light into the dark places and choose to free your spirit of any oppressive old paradigms.

To begin the ritual, I start with cleansing my home and myself with herbs, soaps, incense and healings. Then I meditate, pray & chant mantras to bring forth the masters, saints, angels and spirit guides to assist with the ritual.

WHAT YOU DO:

Then, you will make a list of the things you want to renew, manifest, enhance, or release in or from your life.

Note: *If you are attending a Celebration with other women, bring this list with you to be used during the Fire Ceremony. At that time, you will send it up to the Universe, by burning it in the fire to assist in receiving your desires.*

Take a piece of parchment paper and write a list of everything that you want to let go of from the past year – resentments, habits and behaviours that no longer serve you, limiting beliefs, fears, conflicts, physical or mental conditions.

Then thank all those items on that list for having been with you and for all the lessons learned and ways you grew from them.

Next make a clear statement of letting go such as: I now let go of all these things and anything else that no longer serves me and my miraculous life as I step into a new glorious year."

If you will be doing this at a Celebration later, then save your list for that occasion.

If you are doing this ritual by yourself, or with a friend or family member, then continue following the instructions below.

Gather around a fire (outside, or in a fireplace) and throw the paper in to be burned.

Note: *If you don't have a fireplace, you can CAREFULLY burn it in a large stainless-steel bowl. (Parchment paper does not smoke when burned.)*

Then speak out loud everything you're grateful for from the past year -- the joys, celebrations, accomplishments, lessons learned, and "growth" experiences. Offer those into the fire to be amplified.

And now it's time to call in what you'd like to bring forward in the next year.

Write it out on a piece of paper, then read it out loud ... everything that you welcome into your vision —the intentions, beliefs, behaviours, relationships and everything else that you will embrace.

Offer those into the fire to ignite the new.

Then, put on some music and dance!

Why not make some **FLOWER WREATHS** for yourselves? You can't help but feel the magic with flowers in your hair!

Estelle Reder

PART II: PREPARING THE CEREMONY

n order to prepare for the ceremony, you will need to gather supplies to organize the following:

- The Altar of Summer Solstice

    - The Nature Spirits

- Honouring the Earth Mothers

    - Music Suggestions

Before you focus on the ceremony itself, it is important to set up the altar and the fire. Start with a white clean tablecloth suitable for your altar size. Then, include Red for the altar ... a red candle for each person present. Also add red flowers in a basin filled with water and fragrance (either scented oils and/or rose or other flower petals.

Tools for calling in the direction
- any of the following:
a feather
a white quartz
a drum
a shaker

A cauldron
to seat the red candles

– it can be any metal container
or a flower pot filled almost to the top with sand.

Anointing oil
(see Chapter 9 for details)

Sweetgrass or sage to use for smudge for cleansing, which you will pass around the circle. Incense, drums and instruments, and light for the fire.

Flowers and food for the nature spirits or elementals, who have only one element to their nature – usually air, fire, water or earth. These are the nature spirits that interact with the natural world but have their existence in the ethers.

airies: often found perched in leafy trees, hiding in the knots and furls of ancient trunks, or in the long grass, dipping their toes in the secluded edge of a pond, dancing amidst mushrooms or toadstools, chatting to birds in berry-filled bushes.

Fairies are shy of humans and prefer to have lots of hidden nooks and secluded places where they can conduct their revels in private, away from the prying eyes of humans!

What do fairies eat besides milk, cream, and butter? Fairies love sweets - cakes with milk or cakes and ale can be left out on Summer Solstice.

Elves: Elves were said to be diminutive shape-shifters. (Shakespeare's elves were tiny, winged creatures that lived in, and playfully flitted around flowers.)

English male elves were described as looking like little old men, though elf maidens were invariably young and beautiful. Elves live in kingdoms found in forests, meadows, or hollowed-out tree trunks.

Elves love sugar cookies, syrup and candy canes. They also like all types of food, such as fish or peas. Salad is a real delicacy for them.

Gnomes: Gnomes are also known as 'Earth Spirits', so they are guardians of the animal world. They tend to sick and injured animals and will often release a trapped animal from a human's snare.

A gnome can live up to 400 years, and they survive on a vegetarian diet - nuts, seeds, poppy, mushroom, potatoes, beets, herbal teas, nuts, berries, fruit, mushrooms.

Gnomes give us the basic energy of life in its rawest form. They can help us attract money and fulfill our material needs.

Billions of gnomes tend the earth through the cycles of the four seasons and see to it that all living things are supplied with their daily needs.

They also process the waste and by-products that are an inevitable part of our everyday existence and purge the earth of poisons and pollutants that are dangerous to the physical bodies of man, animal and plant life—including industrial and toxic wastes, pesticides, acid rain, radiation and every abuse of the earth.

On spiritual levels, the gnomes have an even heavier chore. They must clean up the imprints of man kind's discord and negativity that remain at energetic levels in the earth.

War, murder, rape, child abuse, the senseless killing and torture of animals, profit seeking at the expense of the environment as well as hatred, anger, discord, gossip—all these create an accumulation of negatively charged energy that becomes a weight on the earth body and on the nature spirits.

Leprechauns: Leprechauns are Irish red-haired male figures ... less than 24 inches long.

They have pointed ears, red, thick and bushy sideburns and they sometimes have a curly beard on their chin. Their cheeks and nose are rosy most of the time. They wear green hats and green clothing with black leather shoes.

They live in an invisible village, in a forest inside Ireland. Elsewhere, they live in small caves, hollow trees underneath large bushes.

Leprechauns eat wild foods - wildflowers, nuts, potatoes and mushrooms. They enjoy drinking fancy beverages such as dandelion tea.

They love gold coins and four-leafed clovers.

Water spirits or undines: The elementals whose domain is the water element are known as undines.

These beautiful, supple mermaid-like beings are subtle and swift in their movements and can change form rapidly.

The undines control the tides and have much to do with the climate as well as oxygenation and precipitation. The undines cleanse not only the physical waters, but also that aspect of mankind's life that relates to the water element—our emotional and subconscious world.

They carry on their backs the weight of mankind's emotional pollution—feelings that are not at peace, such as anger, emotional abuse, unloving speech, selfishness, anxiety and indulgence.

This is a picture of a Sylph.
It loves you.

Air spirits or sylphs: They are sources of light that produce inspiration and feed the mind. They appear as very ethereal light beings. The sylphs tend the air element, directing the flow of air currents and atmospheric conditions.

They purify the atmosphere and aerate every cell of life with the sacred breath of Spirit. They are bearers of the life-sustaining prana that nourishes all living things.

On subtle levels, the sylphs transmit the currents of the Spirit from heaven to earth.
They can help us with our spiritual and mystical development.

The sylphs often have thin, ethereal bodies that transform gracefully into myriad shapes as they soar through the air. Sylphs are able to travel at great distances very quickly, and giant sylphs can actually span the skies and interpenetrate the earth, the water and the fire elements.

Like giant transformers, sylphs conduct the currents of the mind of God unto the mind of man.

They also work to purify the air of pollutants—everything from car exhaust to toxic fumes emitted from factories and other industrial processes—before these can pollute the water and the earth.

The air element corresponds to the mental level of existence, and thus the sylphs also have the job of purifying the mental plane.

The mental plane can become polluted by negative thoughts that feed hatred, anger, racial prejudice, religious bigotry, resentment, pride, ambition, greed, jealousy and other poisons of the spirit.

Fire spirits or salamanders: The fourth group of elementals work with the fire element and are called salamanders. Their job is crucial, for they serve at the atomic level of all organic and inorganic life, infusing the molecules of matter with the spiritual fires of creation.

The salamanders imbue the entire creation with the energies of the Spirit necessary to sustain life on earth. Capable of wielding both the most intense fires of the physical atom and the purifying, spiritual fires of Spirit, they control the spiritual-material oscillation of light within the nucleus of every atom.

Whether in electricity, firelight or the flame of a candle, the salamanders are agents for the transfer of the fires of the subtle world for mankind's daily use. Without the spark of life sustained by salamanders, life and matter begin to decay, corrode and disintegrate.

The burdens upon the salamanders range from the weight of mankind's hatred to irresponsible uses of nuclear energy. Were it not for the fiery salamanders absorbing and transmuting the huge conglomerates of negativity over the large cities of the world, crime and darkness would be much more advanced than it is today.

The very sustaining of life—the air we breathe, the food we eat, the water we drink—is something most of us take for granted. Yet at the most basic level, we are utterly dependent on the selfless service of the nature spirits.

The miracle of life is the miracle of the gnomes, sylphs, undines and salamanders.

This is the time to honour and thank them for their service to mankind and the planet itself.

Make up your own (small) basket or plate of offerings to them.

Say: *"On this night, we acknowledge the presence of the nature spirits, and welcome*

the visitors to our world – the fairies, elves, leprechauns and other elementals. We ask that you accept our offerings of vegetables, fruit and flowers that we leave here for you on the altar tonight."

Please proceed to lay your offerings on the altar or on the ground around the altar, one by one.

Leave the offerings out overnight and the next day, you can scatter them in a park, forest or crop of trees close by your residence, while expressing gratitude.

Many early societies had a mother-like god form, and honoured the sacred feminine with their ritual, art and legends.

Ancient carvings of rounded, curved, feminine forms found are symbols of something once revered. Pre-Christian cultures like the Norse and Roman societies honoured the deities of women, with their shrines and temples built to honour such goddesses. Those goddesses of motherhood from ancient societies were a widely varied bunch -- some loved unwisely, some fought battles to protect their young, others fought with their offspring.

Here are some of the many mother goddesses found throughout the ages.

- **Asasa Ya (Ashanti):** This earth mother goddess prepares to bring forth new life in the spring, and the Ashanti people honour her at the festival of Durbar, alongside Nyame, the sky god who brings rain to the fields.

- **Bast (Egyptian):** Bast was an Egyptian cat goddess who protected mothers and their newborn children. A woman suffering from infertility might make an offering to Bast in hopes that this would help her conceive.

- **Bona Dea (Roman):** This fertility goddess was worshipped in a secret temple on the Aventine hill in Rome, and only women were permitted to attend her rites. A woman might make a sacrifice to Bona Dea in hopes that she would become pregnant.

· **Brighid (Celtic):** This Celtic hearth goddess was originally a patron of poets and bards but was also known to watch over women in childbirth, and thus evolved into a goddess of hearth and home.

· **Cybele (Roman):** This mother goddess of Rome was at the centre of a rather bloody cult, in which eunuch priests performed mysterious rites in her honour. Her lover was Attis, and her jealousy caused him to castrate and kill himself.

· **Demeter (Greek):** Demeter is one of the best-known goddesses of the harvest. When her daughter Persephone was kidnapped and seduced by Hades, Demeter went straight to the bowels of the Underworld to rescue her lost child. Their legend has persisted for millennia as a way of explaining the changing of the seasons and the death of the earth each fall.

· **Freya (Norse):** A goddess of fertility, abundance and war, she is often associated with sexual freedom. Freya can be called upon for assistance in childbirth and conception, to aid with marital problems, or to bestow fruitfulness upon the land and sea.

· **Frigga (Norse):** Frigga, the wife of the all-powerful Odin, is considered a goddess of fertility and marriage. Like many mothers, she is a peacemaker and mediator in times of strife.

· **Gaia (Greek):** Gaia is known as the life force from which all other beings spring, including the earth, the sea and the mountains. A prominent figure in Greek mythology, Gaia is also honoured by many today as the earth mother herself.

· **Isis (Egyptian):** In addition to being the fertile wife of Osiris, Isis is honoured for her role as the mother of Horus, one of Egypt's most powerful gods, the divine mother of every pharaoh of Egypt, and ultimately of Egypt itself. She assimilated with Hathor, another goddess of fertility, and is often depicted nursing her son Horus. There is a wide belief that this image served as inspiration for the classic Christian portrait of the Madonna and Child.

· **Juno (Roman):** In ancient Rome, Juno was the goddess who watched over women and marriage. As a goddess of domesticity, she is honoured in her role as protector of the home and family.

· **Mary (Christian):** There is a lot of debate about whether or not Mary, the mother of Jesus, should be considered a goddess or not. She is included on this list because she is a Divine figure. For further information on this topic, you may wish to read the book: _Woman Thou Art God_.

· **Yemaya (West African/Yoruban):** This Orisha is a goddess of the ocean and considered the Mother of All. She is the mother of many of the other Orishas and is honoured in connection with the Virgin Mary.

Now that you've been introduced to the many goddesses – pick the one you feel a connection with to perform the following simple ritual.

Note: _This ritual can be adapted for a group easily. You could include it in your Summer Solstice Ceremony, or you could consider doing it as part of a women's circle, in which each member honours the others as part of the rite._

What You Need:

✓ A white candle
✓ An offering
✓ A bowl of water
✓ Pebbles or small stones

Here's How:

This ritual is designed to honour the feminine aspects of the universe as well as our female ancestors. If you have a particular deity you call upon, feel free to change names or attributes around where needed. Otherwise, you can use the all-encompassing name of "Goddess" in the rite.

Decorate your altar with symbols of femininity: cups, chalices, flowers, lunar objects, fish, and doves or swans. You'll also need the following items:

- A white candle
- An offering of something that is important to you
- A bowl of water
- A handful of small pebbles or stones

If your tradition calls for you to cast a circle, do so now. Begin by standing in the goddess position, and saying:

*"I am **(your name),** and I stand before you,*
goddesses of the sky and earth and sea,
I honour you, for your blood runs through my veins, one woman,
standing on the edge of the universe. Tonight, I make an offering in
Your names, as my thanks for all you have given me."

Light the candle and place your offering on the altar. The offering may be something tangible, such as bread or wine or flowers. It can also be something symbolic, such as a gift of your time or dedication. Whatever it is, it should be something from your heart.

Note: *You may want to read up on Offerings to the Gods for some other ideas.*

Once you have made your offering, it is time to call upon the goddesses by name.

Say: *"I am **(your name),** and I stand before you, Mothers of the ancient people, guardians of those who walked the earth thousands of years ago, I offer you this as a way of showing my gratitude.*

Your strength has flowed within me, your wisdom has given me knowledge, your inspiration has given birth to harmony in my soul."

Now it is time to honour the women who have touched your life. For each one, place a pebble into the bowl of water. As you do so, say her name and how she has impacted you. You might say something like this:

*"I am **(your name)**, and I stand before you,*
*to honour the sacred feminine that has touched my heart. I honour **(insert name)** who gave birth to me and raised me to be strong; I honour **(insert name)** my grandmother, whose patience and kindness to strangers taught me to be thoughtful and generous of spirit; I honour **(insert name)** my aunt, who lost her courageous battle with cancer; I honour **(insert name)** my sisters, who have stood by me through thick and thin in this and other lifetimes.*

Continue until you have placed a pebble in the water for each of these women and to any other women whom you wish to honour.

Reserve one pebble for yourself. Finish by saying: *"I am **(your name)**, and I honour myself, for my strength, my creativity, my knowledge, my inspiration, and for all the other remarkable things that make me a woman."*

Take a few minutes and reflect on the sacred feminine. What is it about being a woman that gives you joy? Meditate on the feminine energy of the universe for a while, and when you are ready, end the ritual.

For more information on Celebrating Women's Wisdom, check out the website: Patti Wigington.com

33

Chapter 7: Music Suggestion

This CD is and is very beautiful to listen to before, during or after the ceremony. It is a diverse blend of native cultures on this continent and will captivate your senses. Hopefully, it will also bring you a little closer to nature itself.

While it represents a cross-section of musical influences from different nations, it does feature two authentic prayers in the Cayuga language. These prayers give us a glimpse into the intricate belief system of the Haudenosaunee culture (Mohawk, Oneida, Onondaga, Cayuga and Seneca or people of the longhouse).

One of those is my very favourite and I have used it in every Summer Solstice Celebration that I have hosted, and the following is a brief explanation of it.

GANOHONYOHK
(Thanksgiving Homage)

The Thanksgiving prayer pays homage to the Creator, offering thanks to the Great Spirit and to all other spiritual forces. The Spirit Forces are thanked in order of their age and closeness to Mother Earth.

First, we praise the youngest spirits ... the plants and powerful medicines growing up from the ground, the low-lying fruits and the strawberry (which is a sacrament used in native land ceremonies.)

We honour the bushes and forests and the venerable maple tree. So, too, we revere the animal spirits and the lakes and streams and offer thanks for the food provided by the Great Spirit.

When the Creator was finished making Mother Earth, it is said he created spiritual forces above the earth, appointing them to safe-guard his creation.

And so, we invoke our Grandfathers ... the Thunders, who bring the rains, snow and clear skies,
... our Older Brother, the Sun, who brightens and warms the earth, and
... our Grandmother, the Moon, who rises to grace the night sky alongside the Stars.

We offer thanks to the revealers, the prophets, and to the oldest Spirit Forces: The Four Winds and the Creator of all.

Ganohonyohk. Ganohonyohk. Ganohonyohk.

Thank You.   Thank You.   Thank You.

13 Songs for Summer Solstice – Patheos
www.patheos.com

The theme is fun fire/sun songs that make you want to sing along or dance. There is no particular order. Enjoy and Blessed Solstice to you all!

Pagan wiccan music. summer solstice
katerinaelhaj.bandcamp.com

Paul Winter – Celtic Solstice Music
https://www.amazon.com/Celtic-Solstice

Chants & Songs | Ozark Pagan Mamma
https://tressabelle.wordpress.com

Maggie Sansone   **Celtic Music for the**
Summer Solstice
https://www.brownpapertickets.com

How to celebrate the summer solstice the Irish way |
IrishCentral.com
https://www.irishcentral.com

Of course, there are many other music selections that would be equally suitable, and as all paths are equally valid, so it is with your music selection. Whatever your instincts move you to use is the right choice for your celebration.

PART III: A CELTIC CEREMONY

You will need to decide how long you want the ceremony to take. This is very important, as you don't want to drag it out too long.

So, once you have chosen the different components for your celebration, then you need to time how long each section will take, and on the night of your celebration, it is important to keep to your timed schedule so that it doesn't drag on too long.

While there are no hard and fast rules about the length of the celebration, generally, over the years I have found that starting between 5:30 p.m. to 6:30 p.m. the best, allowing 30 minutes for meet and greet and organizing the celebrants.

I've started my ceremony at 7:00 p.m. and depending on how people are in attendance, some of the components will take longer. I have tried to keep it between 40 to 90 minutes at the maximum, followed by dinner and drinks and socializing ☺

Chapter 8: Casting the Circle
(Option 1 - Goddess)

Y̶ou will always start the ceremony by casting the circle clockwise. Instruct your participants as follows:

Air: Turn to the East.
Arms raised; fingers spread.

"Breath of Goddess, Blow. Be wind in our sails. Be divine mind in ours. Be here in this hour. Blessed Be!"

Fire: Turn to the South.
Arms raised, hands making fists.

"Energy of Goddess, Empower! Be hot within us. Be passion in our hearts. Be here in this hour. Blessed Be!"

Water: Turn to the west.
Arms outstretched; hands cupped.

"Living Waters, blood of Goddess, Flow! Your heartbeat pulses within us. Be dreams and feelings flowing forth. Be here in this hour. Blessed be!"

Earth: Turn to the North.
Arms outstretched, palms down.

"Body of Goddess, Standing stones–dancing bones! Be our strength. Be sacred ground firm under our feet. Be here in this hour. Blessed Be!"

Spirit: Turn to the center.

Hand in hand, thumbs pointing left:

> "From the ground, from the stone,
> From the windswept sky,
> From the flaming fire's cone,
> From the flowing water's sigh,
> Our spirits call, our voices sing
> Of Elemental Power.
> Come, aid us in our circle
> Be here in this hour.
>
> The Circle is cast,
> we are between the worlds
> At the Goddess' feet.
> Where magic is real,
> All becomes one
> and beginnings and endings meet.
> Blessed Be!"

Casting the Circle
(Option 2 – Shamanic)

The opening of this sacred space is essentially an invocation, calling the spirits of the four cardinal directions—South, West, North, and East—and Mother Earth and Father Sky.

Begin by facing the South direction and then each direction in turn, repeating the following procedure:

1. Smudge – fan smoldering sage or incense—or blow scented   water.

2. Then hold your arm up, the palm of your hand facing outward and recite the appropriate verse of the invocation, calling upon the archetype representative of that direction. The archetypes are more than symbols; they are primordial energies or spirits, having qualities and powers of their own.

3. We summon serpent in the South, jaguar in the West, hummingbird in the North and eagle in the East. When summoning Mother Earth, actually touch the ground where you stand; when summoning Father Sky, reach to the heavens.

Prayer for Creating Sacred Space

To the winds of the South
Great serpent,
Wrap your coils of light around us,

Teach us to shed the past
the way you shed your skin,
To walk softly on the Earth.
Teach us the Beauty Way.

To the winds of the West
Mother jaguar,
Protect our medicine space.
Teach us the way of peace,
to live impeccably
Show us the way beyond death.

To the winds of the North.
Hummingbird, Grandmothers and Grandfathers, Ancient Ones
Come and warm your hands by our fires
Whisper to us in the wind
We honour you who have come before us,
And you who will come after us,
our children's children.

To the winds of the East.
Great eagle, condor
Come to us from the place of the rising Sun.
Keep us under your wing.
Show us the mountains
we only dare to dream of.
Teach us to fly wing to wing
with the Great Spirit.

Mother Earth.
We've gathered for the healing
of all your children.
The Stone People, the Plant People.
The four–legged, the two–legged,
the creepy crawlers. the finned,
the furred, and the winged ones.
All our relations.

Father Sun, Grandmother Moon, to the Star nations. Great Spirit,
you who are   known by a thousand names

And you who are the unnamable One.
Thank you for bringing us together.

Casting the Circle
(Option 3 - Pagan)

You can use just a simple invocation in each direction, as follows:

Air, my breath
Hail to the East

Fire, my soul
Hail to the South

Water, life's blood
Hail to the West

Earth, my bones
Hail to the North

Celtic Prayer of St. Patrick (Option 1)

I arise today
through the strength of heaven.
Light of sun,
Radiance of moon,
Power of wind and depth of sea,
Firmness of rock
Stability of the earth.

I arise today,
Part of the unity
between Creator and Creation.
God before me.
God behind me.
God beside me.
God within me.

Pagan Prayer to the Sun (Option 2)

The sun is high above us
shining down upon the land and sea,
making things grow and bloom.

Great and powerful sun,
you are known by many names
Ra, Helios, Sol, Invictus, Aten ...
we honour you this day
and thank you for your gifts.

You are the light over the crops,
the heat that warms the earth,
the hope that springs eternal,
the bringer of life.

We welcome you,
and we honour you this day,
celebrating your light,
as we begin our journey
once more into the darkness.

Chapter 9: Anointing with oil

First, you have to prepare your anointing oil. The process is fairly straightforward, and once the oil is ready, you can use it in a variety of different ways.

You can use plain or scented olive oil, but it should be olive oil either way since it has greater traditional and biblical significance than other types of oil. It is not necessary to buy special oil for anointing.

Extra-virgin cold-pressed olive oil is the purest variety available, so many people prefer to use that when shopping for an anointing oil. You can find this oil in the vast majority of grocery stores. If desired, you can buy scented olive oil from a religious or secular store. Oil that has been perfumed with frankincense and myrrh is both popular and spiritually significant. (Just use 2-3 drops of each.)

Place a small amount of oil in a vial. Find a small vial, bottle, or other container with a tight lid that does not leak. Pour a little olive oil into this container. This will become the anointing oil.
The most common vial is a short metal container with a screw-on lid, with a sponge placed inside to help hold the oil in.

Pray a blessing over the oil. As long as your denomination does not prohibit it, you can usually pray a blessing over the oil on your own and without the help of a religious authority figure. The prayer should be firm and one made in full faith.

The prayer you use must ask God to bless and cleanse the oil, so that it can be used for the sake of God's glory. For instance, the prayer might be something like, "God, I pray that you anoint this oil in Your heavenly name. I pray that You cleanse it of any defilement in it or upon it, and that You make it holy for the work of Your glory. May this be done in the name of the Father, the Son, and the Holy Spirit. Amen."

The best way to keep the oil fresh is to store it sealed and at room temperature. Refrigeration is not recommended – although not harmful, it will start to look cloudy.

Now that you have your anointing oil ready and waiting on the altar, stand before the altar while the participants form a circle around the altar, and will step forward one at a time.

When anointing someone else, wet your right thumb with a little of the anointing oil and use it to draw a cross in the middle of the other person's forehead. while they say ""Open my mind and inner eyes to greater truths."

Next, you will anoint the heart – word of caution ... do not touch the participant's clothing with the oil, as it could cause a permanent stain. Instead, simply make the sign of the cross in the air in front of the participant's heart, while they say, "Cleanse my heart from all impurity."

You will then anoint the hands with oil, making a cross on the inside of each palm, while the participant says, "Let my hands be lifted up in praise, and set to the work of the Goddess."

You will then anoint the feet with oil, making a cross on the top of each foot while the participant says, "Guide my feet on the paths of growth and enlightenment."

Note: You could prepare the following on a 4 x 6 card, or on a full-page (preferably laminated to avoid it smudging.)

Hand the card to the first participant and have them hand it over to the next participant, until you have come full circle. Another option is to make a copy for each participant.

When you are Anointed on the forehead
Say, *"Open my mind and inner eyes to greater truths."*

When you are Anointed on the Heart,
Say, *"Cleanse my heart from all impurity."*

When you are Anointed on the hands,
Say, *"Let my hands be lifted up in praise, and set to the work of the Goddess."*

When you are Anointed on the feet,
Say, *"Guide my feet on the paths of growth and enlightenment."*

Remind your participants that this will not be a quiet circle. This is an exuberant season and it's PARTY TIME! Invoke your wild woman!

Mention that coming up will be a power ritual, to remind us that this season's emphasis is on fulfilment, but that we will also do a banishing as a first reminder of the coming dark season.

Think carefully of what you will ask of the Mother tonight; she is at her highest point of giving. Make sure that what you ask for is what you really, really want!

Chapter 10: Invocation

Charge of the Goddess (Option 1)

Ask all participants to use their drums softly while you say out loud the invocation, as follows:

"This is the fullness of summer, the reign of the Mother Goddess. Tonight, all wants are fulfilled, all wishes come true, and love reaches full passion.

Women everywhere are gathered together to invoke the Goddess. Our many voices embrace her, to awaken her from the long sleep of patriarchy.

Listen to her words...

I have slept for ten thousand years.
Now I stretch and waken.
They are calling, calling me,
and my heart leaps to greet them.

My forests my hair, the grasses my heavy eyelashes. They call me, and I
waken.

My body bedecked with a million flowers,
I want to embrace all the sad and lost,
all the wrongs that have been done,
and make them right.

I am the defender of every mother,
as I am the defender of my holy self.

Earth, Mother am I,
the only one; life springs from me.

I carry the seed of creation.
And I awake!

Everyone says:
Gaia, Carry Us Home!

Invocation of a Reiki Master (Option 2)

Just for today, I will not anger.

Just for today, I will not worry.

Just for today, I will be grateful.

Just for today, I will do my work honestly.

Just for today, I will be kind to every living being.

Chapter 11: Colour Meditation

We are going to do a colour meditation, followed by a spiral dance. As soon as it ends, I will take a hand near me and we will do a spiral dance. As we unwind it, we'll gather in a circle.

Drumming: This should start out as heartbeat and quicken slightly with each change in the meditation.

All women not drumming should take a posture of the five-pointed star.

Keep eyes open and visualize or close them.

BREATHE!

"Feel the movement and heartbeat of the earth at Solstice, feel the rich black earth. Draw black into your body, through your feet, legs, vagina, abdomen, heart, chest, throat, and head. Feel it enter through your feet, travel through your body; feel its vastness and depth, let it exit through the crown. Feel the richness of the Mother Earth.

Feel the colour shift to red, see the pulsing of your blood, the movements of energy and passionate life. Feel your strength, the length of your muscles, the marrow and hardness of your bones.

Now let the colour lighten to a bright warm orange. Feel yourself bathed in energy and power. Feel your body rise in passion, in yearning, in ecstatic union with all that is.

Now let the colour brighten more to an active, vibrant yellow. This is the colour of knowledge and power, of oomph, the bright understanding of things happening, and making them happen. Know yourself to be the cause, the agent of changes. Wash in yellow!

Now let your mind's eye cool a bit and let the green grow and spread out from your heart. This is the colour of sympathy and emotion, of growing and helping things to grow. Green is the colour of healing. Feel the fertile green, where love takes root.

Green shifts cooler now, to blue. Blue is the colour of the sky, the water. It is the colour of will, peace, and the natural order. Let your will be in harmony, let your throat be filled with songs and the words you need to say. Know that yours is the power to make real that which you imagine.

Feel the colour purple now, the colour of psychic knowing. Let the winds whisper, the fire burns within, the waters of intuition flow, and the secrets be known to you. Know what you know and be unafraid.

Let all the colours swirl faster and faster about you and through you until they make a swirling white light, around you and in you. This is the colour of the Goddess, of the great Divine one. You are part of Her, of all of it. Feel the patterns moving, the wheel is turning, turning, see the light of it, be en-light-en-ment."

Chapter 12: Spiral Dance

The leader will start by holding the next person's hand, and while spiraling, chant one line and have everyone repeat after you the following chant:

(Leader) We are the music in everyone.
(All) We are the music in everyone.

(Leader) We are the dance of the moon and the sun.
(All) We are the dance of the moon and the sun.

(Leader) We are the power in everyone.
(All) We are the power in everyone.

(Leader) We are the hope that will not die.
(All) We are the hope that will not die.

(Leader) And we are the turning of the tide.
(All) And we are the turning of the tide.

(Leader) Air I am.
(All) Air I am.
(Leader)Fire I am.
(All) Fire I am.

(Leader) Water, Earth and Spirit I am.
(All) Water, Earth and Spirit I am.

As you move back into one big circle, each person takes a candle from the altar.

Start by lighting the first candle, then state your wish.

Light candles from each other, going deosil (clockwise), one at a time and stating your wish.

Now go around again, widdershins (counter-clockwise.)

This time state a banishing and blow your candle out.

When all candles are out, go back and light candles at the altar, saying,

"On this night, the Goddess grants all wishes. Blessed be!"

Place candles in the cauldron sand and let them burn until it is time to go.

Chapter 13: Closing the Circle

Turn to each direction in reverse order:

North: Great Spirits of the North, Spirits of Earth, we thank you for your presence. It is done. Go if you wish, stay if you will. Blessed Be!

West: Great Spirits of the West, Spirits of Water, we thank you for your presence. It is done. Go if you wish, stay if you will. Blessed Be!

South: Great Spirits of the South, Spirits of Fire, we thank you for your presence. It is done. Go if you wish, stay if you will. Blessed Be!

East: Great Spirits of the East, Spirits of Air, we thank you for your presence. It is done. Go if you wish, stay if you will. Blessed Be!

Turn to the centre, join hands:

By the Earth that is Her body, the Air that is her breath, by the Fire of Her bright spirit, and the Waters of her living womb, The Circle is closed but unbroken. (Drop hands.)

May the peace of the Goddess go in our hearts, as we merry meet, merry part, and merry meet again.

Blessed Be!

PART IV: SHAMANIC CEREMONY

I f you are a Shaman or have a leaning towards shamanic teachings, this is a sample of one option for a summer solstice event. If this doesn't interest you, skip to the next chapter for other options.

Unless a Circle is already part of some ongoing shamanic tradition with traditional Solstice ceremonies, it is usually best for a Circle to journey and discover what ceremonies and celebrations to do.

Just as individuals are learning from their helping Spirits new ways of doing shamanic healing, special dances and songs, so also Circles can learn from Spirits new ceremonies appropriate to them and to this time in which we live.

With the thought that some Circles might not have done Solstice Ceremonies before, here are some suggestions of how you might focus your intentions as you plan your activities.

Generally speaking, shamanic Summer Solstice Ceremonies focus on the themes of fulfillment, enlightenment, abundance, sharing, and the joy of living on this beautiful Earth Home.

These are examples of journeys for what to do once you have gathered, prepared your place of gathering, called upon the Spirits to join you, and created the container within which to do your Circle ceremonial activities.

Again, we suggest journeying before the Solstice so that you can then include what you are shown in your Solstice gathering.

Some of the suggested journeys for ceremonies have as their focus:

1) Honouring the Light ... both within and without ... how can you increase the healing Light of each individual in your Circle?

2) Doing a Fire ceremony that honours the gift of Fire. Fire partakes of the Sun and it is acknowledged as the Sun within the Earth.

3) How can you as an individual and your Circle increase in your vitality and what activities can you do together (drumming, chanting, dancing) that give of your vitality to Earth and other beings.

4) Making a Prayer Stick or Prayer Tree upon which you place specific prayers for those who need healing, for the return to peace where there is no peace, for abundance in areas of the world where there is now poverty and scarcity.

5) How to absorb the beneficent power and strength from the Earth and Sun into your minds, bodies, hearts and souls just as are the plants, animals and other beings now drawing power and strength during this time.

Once you've done this drawing upon the power and strength available, ask for you and your Circle to be filled with the light and enlightenment needed to grow spiritually.

6) Creating a Circle that sends healing love to others round the Earth.

Circling together, find a way consciously to send your blessings and your love in such a way that you see "what you are sending" as encircling the globe of Earth.

One of the most important things to remember about ceremony is that it is a way for humans to give back to Creation some of the energy and blessings that we are always receiving.

Mother Earth constantly gives us two-legged and other creatures a surface on which to place our feet. The Sun's warmth provides the heat necessary for all living beings to prosper.

The relationship of Earth, Sun, and Moon is the matrix within which all living beings evolve during their sojourn here on Earth.

All ceremonies bring an awareness of this Unity with the larger Web of Being and Becoming. "As Above, so Below" and "As without, so within" reflect the understanding that ceremonies are most powerful when the intention and the purpose of the ceremony is to align ourselves with what is occurring within the larger Web, the greater Pattern.

Just as the Solstice signifies the time when Mother Earth is at the fullness of her strength, fertility, and abundance, so we too can celebrate the strength in joining together, pollinate our spiritual consciousness through sharing, and do ceremonies of thanksgiving for the abundance in which we partake daily.

We can offer prayers for those who go without the body's essentials for shelter, food, and nourishment for their spirits. Prayers for those caught up in our human conflicts that lead to war, exile, and disintegration.

Seek guidance from our Spirit helpers and with our Circles on how we might bring more prospering to All.

Celebrate! Celebrate! Celebrate!

Living in a Shamanic Ceremonial and Sacred Way

May our Ceremonies
Our songs, our dances, our prayers
our fires, our breath,
our rattling and drumming
be golden filaments
stretching and tied in one
with other Circles
With the Great Mountains
with the Great Trees,
with the Great Waters,
with the Great Sun,
with the Great Moon,

May our Ceremonies
be golden filaments stretching
tied in one with other Circles
from the Land of the Rising Sun
through the Land of Standing Sun
to the Land of Setting Sun
and all the Lands Betwixt and Between.

May all the Spirits help us
May the Day Sun
May the Night Sun
May All That Is
All That Is
See us, Hear Us,
Witness Us
As One with this World
One with the Road
Going on Forever
and the Ceremonies
Never Ending on this Path.

Blessing! Blessing! Blessing!
One with this World
So May We Be.

Chapter 14: Calling in the Four Directions

This blessing to create sacred space calls upon the four directions as an invocation where we ask for permission to the spirits to do our intentional work.

We call in the spirits of the four cardinal directions and beyond: South, West, North and East, Mother Earth and Father Sky.

To begin, take some deep breaths, let go of any mental preoccupations and align with your heart's intention to create sacred space.

Feel free to change any of the words to align with your vision as this works best when it's authentic to you.

As you face the South, smudge or fan sage or incense, blow scented water, or shake a rattle and repeat the prayer for the South.

Have one arm held up and face the palm of your hand out to receive. Then repeating west, north and east.

When calling in mother earth or "Pachamama" place one hand to the ground and when calling to Father Sky, reach for the stars.

South: To the Winds of the South.

Great Serpent Mother of the Life-giving waters. Wrap your coils of light around us. Remind us how to let go and shed old ways of being. Teach us to walk the way of beauty.

West: To the Winds of the West.

Mother Jaguar. Support me as we see our own fears. Teach us how to transform our fears into love. Remind us how to live with impeccability. May we have no enemies in this lifetime or next.

North: To the Winds of the North Royal Hummingbird Ancient Ones Teach us about your endurance and your great joy Come to us in the dreamtime. With honour we greet you.

East: To the Winds of the East.

Eagle or Condor. Great visionary, remind us to lead from our pure heart. Teach us to soar to new places, to fly wing to wing with Spirit.

Mother Earth- Pachamama we pray for your healing Let us soften into your wisdom

May we take great care of you so that our children and our children's children may witness the beauty and abundance you offer us today

Father Sun, Grandmother Moon, to the Star Nations: Guide us on our journey of discovery, healing and deep connection with nature. Great Spirit- you who are known by a thousand names, and you who are the unnamable One. Thank you for bringing us here at this time.

Chapter 15: Opening of the Seven Chakras

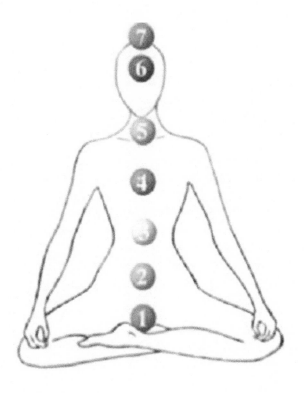

Tap seven times to "AOM" sound,
starting with:

First or Base (Root) Chakra (Red)
Life, Strength & Survival

Second or Naval Chakra (Orange)
Universal Order, Balance & Creativity

Third or Solar Plexus Chakra (Yellow)
Wisdom and Knowledge

Fourth or Heart Chakra (Green)
Love, Forgiveness, Healing & Peace

Fifth or Throat Chakra (Sky Blue)
Power, Enthusiasm & Expression

Sixth or Third Eye Chakra (Royal Blue)
Understanding, Imagination & Intuition

Seventh or Crown Chakra (Purple)
Spiritual Center

Chapter 16: Preparing for the Fire Ceremonies

The mystery of fire lies in the way that it transmutes energy into light and warmth. Fire can cleanse, nurture and refine when properly respected and used.

Acknowledging that life experiences change us, we consciously choose to release what no longer serves and to invoke the energy of positive change for what is to come. In this way we celebrate with Fire the Great Mystery that is Lie and our transformation on the path.

For thousands of years our ancestors have marked the seasons of the year with celebration. These celebrations have served as a way for the communities of the earth to renew themselves and to bond once again with nature and give thanks.

This can be our gift of renewal and transformation, our time to listen and be with the rhythms of nature, and our opportunity to express our gratitude for the gifts of light, love and life.

In preparation for the Fire Ceremony

For this exercise, your participants will need parchment paper, available at any dollar store, grocery store or at Walmart. Parchment has traditionally been used instead of paper for important documents such as religious texts, public laws, and diplomas as it has always been considered a strong and stable material. Everything from the Magna Carta to the U.S. Constitution was written on parchment,

Parchment Paper is a durable material, once made out of the skin of a sheep or goat. The paper can be described as thick, tough, resistant to grease and dirt stains, and does well withstanding water.

A scroll also known as a roll, is a roll of papyrus, parchment, or paper containing writing to convey a theme of antiquity & importance.

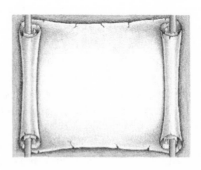

Ideal for writing with ink & pen.
Parchment paper also burns clean with little flying residue.

It is highly suggested that participants spend some quiet time by themselves prior to the ceremony to do this. However, parchment paper will be available on site. If you need it, please come earlier (between 6:00 p.m. and 7:00 p.m. in order to have some quiet time to yourself to complete this task.

Note: *This is the most important part of the ceremony. Do not rush this. Pick a time when you won't be interrupted to meditate or just sit quietly by yourself with a piece of parchment paper and pen by your side, and as thoughts come through, write them down immediately.*

Start by writing down all the aspects of your life that has gone well for you during the year, all that you wish to give thanks for, the goals you have achieved, the new experiences you have gone through, the people in your life who have helped you grow, the help you have received from your celestial guides ... and anything else you can think of.

Then, write down all the aspects of your life that hasn't gone so well for you during the year. From that list, we're going to concentrate on a painful memory or experience ... something or someone who has caused you mental pain, deep sorrow, someone you have been unable to forgive, an experience that caused you great suffering.

You breathe in the pain. You acknowledge and accept the pain you are feeling at that very moment. The main point is that the suffering should be real, totally heartfelt, tangible, honest, and vivid.

Write this experience on parchment paper putting down all your feelings. Be as thorough and explicit as you can. You're the only one that will read this, and then it will be offered to God in the Burning Ceremony.

After you're finished writing, sit back and take some deep breathes, breathing out kindness, compassion and forgiveness - whatever you feel would lighten your load.

Then, roll your parchment paper up in a scroll, tie it up with a brightly coloured ribbon and bow or flower. It can be as simple or as ornate as you want it to be.

A Pole God-Image

Wooden figurines, sometimes called pole gods, have been found at many archaeological sites in Central and Northern Europe. They are generally interpreted as depicting deities, sometimes with either a votive or an apotropaic (protective) function.

The majority are more or less crudely worked poles or forked sticks; some take the form of carved planks. The Old Norse term has a homonym meaning "pole" or "beam".

As the origin of the "god word" and the etymology was accepted by some scholars; it would suggest that the word is derived from god-images in pole form.

Based on this premise, you could make your own god-image in pole form, to bring as a gift to feed the fire. This could be as simple as a stick (or two or more) decorated with moss, ribbons, flowers, or whatever comes to mind– use your creativity and imagination and have fun with it!

This gift represents your hopes and dreams, to give thanks, express your fears, anger, beliefs - let the fire symbolically transform and transmute them. The following are some ideas done by past participants -it can be simple or ornate.

Chapter 17: The Fire Ceremonies

Father God (fire) – Mother Azna (water)

Father God and Mother Azna, we acknowledge with gratitude your gifts of light, love and life.

We give thanks to you on this night, for your constant guidance, assistance, love and protection.

In return, we ask that you accept this gift made from Mother Earth that we now burn in your honour. representing our dreams, thanks, fears, anger, and beliefs.

Let the fire symbolically transform and transmute them.

Please proceed to toss into the fire your earth image.

The Intention Burning Ceremony

Now, we will present our scrolls to the fire, with the following intent:

Say out loud: *"The light of the Higher Power is now bringing to light that which should not be hidden. I am willing to look at those secrets within me or within my world that are now being brought to light.*

My Highest Self is now revealed and I have the strength to know my Highest Self and to be my Highest Self at all times. No circumstances or influence can keep me from knowing and living the love, freedom and power that I am."

Everyone ... form a big circle around the fire.

The circle will move counter-clockwise.

As your turn approaches the fire, pray to God to accept your offering on this Intention.

Release it to God in light & love.

Throw it in the fire.

Estelle Reder

Holding hands, repeat this blessing after me:

Blessing (Guatemalan)

The peace of the earth be with you,
The peace of the heavens, too.

The peace of the rivers be with you,
The peace of the oceans, too.

Deep peace falling over you.
God's peace growing in you.

The peace of the mountains be with you,
The peace of the valleys, too.

The peace of the forests be with you,
The peace of the prairies, too.

Deep peace falling over you.
God's peace growing in you.

Chapter 18: Closing the Four Directions (Option 1: Shamanic)

It is important to close the space when you have finished your ceremony. When you close sacred space, you again address the elements and spirit helpers. Thanking them for keeping your space open, for keeping you focused and protected, and for their love and wisdom that they shared with you during this sacred time.

To close the space, follow the same procedure as for the opening, acknowledging the four directions, Mother Earth and Father Sky. Thank the archetypes for being with you—serpent, jaguar, hummingbird, and eagle—and release their energies to return to the four corners of the Earth, as follows:

To the winds of the South
Great Serpent.
Thank you for the healing light you bring to us. For helping us to shed the deadness of our pasts - the way you shed your skin - all at once. Thank you for your wisdom in teaching us the Beauty Way.

To the winds of the West
Mother Sister Jaguar.
Thank you for protecting our medicine space. We embrace your wisdom of teaching us the ways of peace, impeccability, and the journey beyond death.

To the winds of the North
Hummingbird, Grandmothers and Grandfathers - Ancient Ones.

Thank you for sharing this space with us. We listen for your whispers of wisdom to us in the wind and to the sacred space within our hearts. Guide us with your grace.

To the winds of the East
Great Eagle, Condor.

Thank you for taking us upon your wings to our highest path of destiny.   Thank you for showing us the holy mountains and for reminding us to envision our lives from this place.

Mother Earth - Pachamama

We give you thanks, as one of your children, for your wisdom and for holding us so sweetly in your womb of love and life as we heal all of our stories, our shadows, our fears.

Father Sun, Grandmother Moon, Star Nations –
Star Brothers and Sisters, Great Spirit

You who are known by a thousand names - the unnamable, the nameless one. You who are unknown, yet not unknowable. Thank you for bringing us together and allowing us to sing the song of Life one more day.

As you release their energies back to their four directions, take a few deep breaths, acknowledge yourself back in the space you are in and witness any changes in your being.

Take any inspiration gleaned from your sacred space and share them with the earth, your family and your community.

Closing the Four Directions
(Option 2: Goddess)

By the air that is her breath.
By the fire of her bright spirit.
By the waters of her womb.
By the earth that is her body.

Our circle is open. But unbroken.
May the peace (love, joy) of the Goddess
Be ever in our hearts.

Merry meet.
And merry part.
And merry meet again ...

Closing Prayer

Divine Light,
help me to see the way forward
with love, light and joy.

Show me how best to help others,
As well as myself.

Let me spread your Divine Light
Through myself and others,
Without judgement,
conditions or expectations

Amen.

Note*: The "Official Ceremony" is now over
and it is time to celebrate
with food, drink and song.
Go for it!*

PART V: THE INVITATION LIST

O nce you have built your celebration from the many different components available, decide on the number of attendees that your place of celebration can hold comfortably. List the people that you wish to invite. This is usually a women-only event.

The list can be as little as three or as many as 21, keeping in mind the venue and how many can be comfortably accommodated. Anywhere from 3 to 6 to 9 to 12 to 15 to 18 to 21 (multiples of 3's works best for the energy to build and flow).

1. _____

2. _____

3. _____

4. _____

5. _____

6. _____

7. _____

8. _____

9. _____

10. _____

11. _____
12. _____

13. _____
14. _____
15. _____

16. _____
17. _____
18. _____

19. _____
20. _____
21. _____

Chapter 19: Invitation to an Early Dinner

Dinner served before the Celebration (Option 1)

Date: (insert date)
Time: (insert time)
Place: (insert address)
Phone: (insert phone)

Meet and greet at 5:00 p.m.
Potluck dinner at 5:30 p.m.
Fire ceremony will start around 7:30 p.m.
Non-alcoholic fruit punch, beverages and wine
will be supplied complements of the host(s)
before and after the ceremony.

Please confirm attendance by (insert date)
by emailing (insert e-mail address)
Attendees are asked to bring a food contribution.
and advise what category/type of dish you will be bringing
(make a dish for 6-8 people):

Appetizer
Salad
Main dish
Dessert
Or call for further information.

Invitation to a Late Dinner

(Option 2 –Served After the Ceremony)

Date: (insert date)
    Registration: 6:30 p.m.
    Program Starts at: 7:00 p.m.
    Place: (insert address)
    Phone: (insert phone number)

    (optional)
    Collection: $10.00 at Registration
    for (state charity proceeds will go to)

    Celebration with food and wine after the ceremony (after 8:00 p.m.).
    Please contribute to this celebration by bringing a dish to share.

    Please confirm attendance by (insert date)
    by emailing (insert email address) or call
    should you require further information.
Then, include background information as provided next

Note to participants:

1. Bring a drum, or shakers, or two sturdy sticks around 12" long.
2. Food and drink will follow the ceremony in celebration.
3. The ceremony will take place outside (weather permitting).
4. Bring lawn chairs (or lawn chairs will be provided)

5.Do bring a blanket or sweater or jacket (depending on the weather, of course).

6.A small offering (a few) for the nature spirits -gifts of veggies, citrus fruits, sweets, milk or honey.

7.A few flowers and herbs from among the following: Marigold, Daisy, Lavender, Roses, Sunflower, Ivy, St John's Wort, Vervain, Rosemary.

8.Bring one or two candles in any of these colours: Green, Yellow, Gold, Red, and Blue.

9.Bring incense: Lemon, Frankincense, Rose, Myrrh or Pine are some of the suggested incense that work best.

10. Wear summery, yellow coloured clothing or jewelry with sun symbols (any gemstones green or yellow in colour) or wear a flower in your hair.

11. Sage and/or tobacco (optional) to throw in the fire, along with your intentions.

We will have a bonfire outside or candles inside (if weather is not good). In Ancient Pagan times, they used such bonfires to leap over to encourage fertility and prosperity. We won't be leaping ... we'll just walk around the bonfire!

We will make a stick figure using branches and twigs from the ground, wrap ivy and flowers into it; then burn it in the bonfire, whilst giving thanks to God. You can either make your own ahead of time, or supplies will be available on-site to make one that night.

Bring your open heart to hear and connect with the heartbeat (rhythm) of the earth.

Come and get in touch with the awe-inspiring sacred planet we call home. Mother Earth.

Note: If you wish to provide more information to your invitees, you can include a brief recap of why you want them to celebrate with you. You can use some (or all) of the following information,

Litha (pronounced Leetha) is also known as the Summer Solstice or Midsummer; and is the longest day of the year. It is the festival of the Sun's rebirth and a time to honour God where he is at his strongest, highest and brightest. It is a time of celebrating the fertility of the land and the abundance of the earth.

The Summer Solstice celebrates the joy, warmth and laughter of summer; and God's power. The beginning of summer represents a time for purification, renewal of the self, a time to release the sadness, fears and pains from your life. A time for purification and renewed energy.

It is also believed that it is the time of the Faery (fairies) elves, leprechauns, etc. where they come out in great numbers to visit our world. You can welcome them on this day by leaving an offering for them out in your garden (gifts of sweets, milk or honey).

Summer Solstice is a time of gathering of family and tribe. It is a time to celebrate the feminine – the ability to endure and to create. It is a time of healing when we cleanse to make ourselves stronger; when we ask for blessings to prevent tragedy and to protect us and our projects and crops for another year. This is a time of abundance for the first of the harvest – lettuce, green onions, peas, beans, and herbs are now ready.

This year, the next big burst of feminine energy hits the Earth at Midsummer's Eve on (insert date). The feminine is about creating, caretaking, teaching, and love. It is about healing the hurts of the humans and the Earth.

Many will be called to take their places as caretakers and guides for the planet at this Solstice. There will be a profound sense of peace and rightness for those that are called. The feminine is about 'natural' so the organizations and the people that are in unnatural states, may begin breaking down at this time. A profound time of healing will result from this catalyst of energy.

The Sun now exerts its maximum power upon our part of the Earth as its rays strike us head-on. The time of full outward physical manifestation is here. The powers of inner contemplation are at their lowest point, and everywhere are the energies of "doing," of exerting the will.

It is just as true for us today. As we experience the warm, full power of the Solstice Sun, we are called to make true on earth the words of the Master Jesus, "I and the Father are One." To understand this is to recognize the divinity in everyone we meet. Use this day to see God in each face that you greet.

At this time, God represents the element of Fire and the Goddess represents the element of water. We will make offerings to God by decorating the altar with flowers, sun symbols, offerings of seasonal citrus fruits, etc. Not to forget the Goddess, we will also have a bowl of water on the altar.

Fire Ceremony

There will be a Fire Ceremony, allowing each participant an opportunity to let go of something and throw it in the fire .... This is a time to let go of something that has weighed you down long enough. You now wish to give it to the Goddess and God.

It is also time to set an intention and offer a service for the granting of the intention. It is also an auspicious time to declare your love for someone else.

There will be a round for each person to set an intention and offer a "service" ... either service in some capacity, or a blessing/prayer for someone needing support.

Come prepared with what you want to give up and what you want to intend. You may bring sage or tobacco to throw into the fire to strengthen your wish (optional).

One of the most important things to remember about ceremony is that it is a way for humans to give back to Creation some of the energy and blessings that we are always receiving.

Mother Earth constantly gives us two-legged's and other creatures a surface on which to place our feet. The Sun's warmth provides the heat necessary for all living beings to prosper. The relationship of Earth, Sun, and Moon is the matrix within which all living beings evolve during their sojourn here on Earth. All ceremonies bring an awareness of this Unity with the larger Web of Being and Becoming.

"As above, so below" and "As without, so within" reflect the understanding that ceremonies are most powerful when the intention and the purpose of the ceremony is to align ourselves with what is occurring within the larger Web, the greater Pattern.

Just as the Solstice signifies the time when Mother Earth is at the fullness of her strength, fertility, and abundance, so we too can celebrate the strength in joining together, pollinate our spiritual consciousness through sharing, and doing ceremonies of thanksgiving for the abundance in which we partake daily.

We can offer prayers for those who go without the body's essentials for shelter, food, and nourishment for their spirits. Prayers for those caught up in our human conflicts that lead to war, exile, and disintegration. Seek guidance from our Spirit helpers and with our Circles on how we might bring more prospering to All.

As it is also the time of celebrations and socializing ... so wear summery, yellow coloured dresses or clothing and jewelry with sun symbols or wear a flower in your hair.

If you can't join our celebration, wherever you are, find a way to honour Summer Solstice this year – feast with friends, meditate, talk to the Goddess, talk to Great Spirit, or walk in the woods and talk with Mother Earth.

Preparing Yourself for the Summer Solstice Celebration

O n your own, write on some parchment paper all the aspects of your life that has gone well for you during the year.

Then write down all the aspects of your life that hasn't gone so well for you during the year... a list of things that didn't go so well or didn't happen, or things that we need to get off our chest and heart ... any family issues that are unresolved, any person that you can't seem to forgive ... end the list with a big Thank You, God".

No one will see this list but you, and then it will be thrown in the fire and burned right in front of our eyes...going straight up to God. No request too trivial."

If you don't have time to do this ahead of time, or don't have parchment paper, come earlier ... any time after 4:00 p.m. and you can do it in a quiet corner of the house or garden.

We will meditate and thank the Goddess for all that has come to fruition then continue to meditate and ask God to purify and help bring to fruition what goals have not worked during the year.

Finally, we will throw the parchment paper into the fire as the ceremony will take place outside (weather permitting). or burn it with a red candle (if this is an inside event). You may bring sage or tobacco to throw into the fire to strengthen your wish (optional).

- Beforehand, on your own, make a stick figure of God using branches and twigs from the ground, wrap ivy and flowers in it... This will be burnt in the bonfire, whilst giving thanks to God.

- Bring a small dish of fruits and/or veggies from the earth. A few flowers from the list detailed above. (Two or three is sufficient).

- Although we have chairs available, please bring your own lawn chair, if possible.

- Shakers and rattles are encouraged. Drummers are welcome!

- Fast for at least three hours prior to the ceremony.

- Wear summery, yellow coloured clothing or jewelry with sun symbols (any gemstones green or yellow in colour) or wear a flower in your hair.

- Do bring a blanket/sweater or jacket (depending on the weather, of course). Water will be available during the ceremony. Food and drink will follow the ceremony in celebration.

As Summer Solstice warms and blesses us, and fireflies delight us under the twilight of the changing evening sky, we will affirm the magnificence that is the gift of a community of women.

Together we will connect and reflect as we embrace the divine feminine. We will bless our bodies as sacred temples of beauty, creativity and love!

Come sisters!
Come sing and dance in the circle of women!

Bring your open heart to hear and connect with the heartbeat (rhythm) of the earth. Come and get in touch with the awe-inspiring sacred planet we call home ... Mother Earth.

Come gather with your community of sisters.
COME CELEBRATE!

APPENDIX 1: AFFIRMATIONS

You may also be interested in doing some affirmations that would enhance the ritual as well as your life ... affirmations such as:

- I can reprogram any thought that I want to.
- I love all of my body, exactly as it is.
- I love all of me in every way.
- I love everyone unconditionally.
- Everything in my life is exactly as it should be.
- Every day, in every way, the world is becoming more and more wonderful.
- Every single experience I have enriches me and helps me to grow.
- I choose everything that happens to me in life.
- I choose my reactions to everything that happens and I can change those reactions if I wish.
-
-
-

Add your own affirmations, ensuring that the statement is always in the positive, not the negative. Affirming in the positive is very important for reprogramming your thinking process.

APPENDIX 2: ABOUT THE AUTHOR

Estelle is a healer, life coach, author and public speaker. She is a tarot card reader, certified by the Fraser/McLaren Tarot Institute and a Reiki Master/Teacher.

She has studied many alternative healing methods including Cranio-Sacral, Body Reading, light massage, aromatherapy, aura reading, chakra clearing and re-energizing and teaches Reiki, Cranio-Sacral, meditation and aura reading.

Estelle was born and raised in St. Malo, Manitoba and is the seventh child of twelve. She moved to Winnipeg at the age of 17 to pursue her studies and had a fulfilling and varied career for 42 years, working as a professional trainer in both official languages with both the federal and provincial governments.

She also developed and presented training sessions for private businesses and is an inspirational speaker. Her highly interactive seminars involve participants directly in hands-on learning and personal growth. Her company – Estellereder.com – is based on the belief that her clients' needs are of the utmost importance and for the past twenty years, she has devoted her life to assisting clients reach their fullest potential.

That's My Story
Taking a Courageous Path
Book 1 of a Trilogy

An Inspirational Tale of One Woman's Voyage of Self-Discovery, this book shares the spiritual journey of a woman who recognized that the time for a change in her life had finally arrived.

Change presents the greatest opportunity for growth and for author Estelle Reder, it was the catalyst for the inspiring events that enriched her life more than she could have ever hoped.

Led by her angels and spirit guides, she was able to move through the healing and rejuvenation process of the mind, to the spiritual awareness of her life's purpose.

"I started working on this, my first book That's My Story, Book 1, in the year 2000, after many of my friends and students encouraged me to write my story.

Some of my colleagues have likened my books to the same genre as I Give You My Life: The Autobiography of a Western Buddhist Nun, by Ayya Khema, while others have seen some similarities to the works: Stand Up for Your Life, Take Time for Your Life, and Life Makeovers, author Cheryl Richardson as well as Writing for my Life, author Nancy Levin.

This is the first book in a trilogy, with a timely message addressing today's social needs. That's My Story will resonate with individuals from all walks of life. The choices you make change your life."

Available on Amazon. ca and Amazon.com
ISBN: 987-1-63135-147-1 (Paperback)
ISBN: 978-1-62212-992-8 (eBook)

That's My Story
Moving Down a Courageous Path
Book 2 of a Trilogy

This is the second book in the trilogy: That's My Story. Partly memoir, love story, poetry anthology, meditation guide and lesson manual, this book uses a variety of methods to lead the reader down a spiritual path towards inner peace and life miracles.

Health is wealth. We all know that. When health eludes us, we need to find new direction and step out of our comfort zone. The body is trying to tell us something. Pointers gleaned from the path of another may become our stepping stones.

So it is with health and relationships. As humans, we tend to repeat old patterns. To find new happiness, we need to open up to new possibilities. "I can alter my life by altering the attitude of my mind." Moving Down will inspire you to M-O-V-E D-O-W-N your own path with love and to L-O-V-E.

"Your story helps to support those in their awakening by giving them the opportunity to assess the value of the guidance offered and how that aligns with what they already know to be true. It is important to encourage each and all to engage in their own practices that cover their entire being – body, mind, heart and soul. That's the message that the world needs."

~ *Babaji, prophet, guru and avatar*

Available on Amazon.ca and Amazon.com
or through the Publisher's website:
FriesenPress. http://www.friesenpress.com
ISBN: 978-1-4602-3422-8 (Hardcover
ISBN: 987-1-4602-3423-5 (Paperback)
ISBN: 978-1-4602-3423-2 (eBook)

That's my Story
Fully Engaged on a Courageous Path
Book 3 of a Trilogy

Unexpected things come your way in life. It's inevitable. And how you handle them defines you and makes or breaks you. You can learn from your experiences and move forward without repeating the same old patterns of behaviour.

For author Estelle Reder, that journey evolved though a series of exciting new experiences from shamanic journeys to Reiki healings and teachings and guidance from a variety of mystics both earth-bound and celestial.

"There are an increasing number of souls who are awakening to the depths of their own sacred natures. They will resonate with your writing. You deliver these deep messages in a language that is inviting." ~ *Babaji, prophet, guru and avatar*

"Your writing is a beautiful gift. Your books were worth the wait. You truly are a word whisperer."
   ~ *Bonnie Yvonne Bodnarchuk, Artist*

"This, the final book in Estelle's That's My Story trilogy, has been anticipated with much eagerness and wholly satisfies. Her voice is strong, clear and inspirational as she effortlessly weaves a fascinating narrative with inspiration. She reminds us of the truth of who we really are and the steps we need to take to create the life we desire. This is her strength as a writer and story-teller."

   ~ *Marianne Gillis, author, Musings on a Bookshelf: Buddhism to Spiritualism*

"This journey surpassed my wildest hopes. It has profoundly transformed and inspired me. The ripples continue to travel inwards and outwards as I work to integrate these experiences into my life."   ~ *Estelle Reder.*

Available at Amazon.com
or through the Publisher's website:
FriesenPress. http://www.friesenpress.com
ISBN: 978-1-5255-1663-4 (Hardcover)
ISBN: 978-1-5255-1664-1 (Softcover)
ASIN: B07BHYVPXT (eBook)

Auras 101
See and Read Auras in Ten Easy Steps

This book is packed with incredibly easy ways for someone to open themselves up to seeing auras – to get you aura reading. It shows you how to do an aura cleansing and how to keep your aura healthy. If your aura is healthy, your body will be healthy.

Have you ever wondered why - when you go to a mall or other venue where you are in close contact with many people – you come back home exhausted?

If your aura is extended too far out from your body, other people passing by will "steal your energy from your aura."

Because you are not willingly giving your energy to another – it depletes your energy.

This book shows you how to measure your aura and see how far your aura extends; how to revitalize, strengthen and protect your aura. I have included a simple meditation to balance and harmonize your aura.

It is a fun book, filled with simple and easy ways to start seeing and reading your aura.

Available at Amazon.com
ISBN-13: 978-1521782439 (Softcover)
ISBN-10: 1521782431 (eBook)

**Unleash Your Goddess
And Unchain Your Heart**

This book starts out with the signing of a contract with your goddess within, in order to be in complete harmony with your spiritual self. Signing this contract signifies your commitment to change or tune-up your awareness.

You will learn how to unleash your goddess within, as well as how to contact angels through a guided meditation and affirmations.

Many people are afraid to ask, or don't know what or how to ask for help. This book will help you begin to explore specifically what your true desires are.

Keep the following general points in mind as you reflect on what your wants and dreams. Remember, it is never too late to change.

You can be reborn at any time. Every moment is the beginning of a new life. We all have the power of choice. Your goddess within you simply activates this power...or communicates to you its presence and accessibility.

This book provides you with step-by-step methods to Unleashing Your Goddess, Unchaining Your Heart and find your true purpose.

Available at Amazon.com
ISBN-13: 978-1549670237 (Softcover)
ASIN: B0764PQP7D (eBook)

Attracting Love and Romance

I n this book, you will learn how to prepare yourself physically through opening your heart and root chakras. You will learn how to ask the Universe for what you really, really want in a soul mate.

You will be able to follow easy step-by-step instructions on how to prepare your house and bedroom for love and romance, through Feng Shui.

This book will show you how to attract the best person in your life, through a Chakra Meditation, and you will learn how to get your subconscious mind to support your heart's desire. This book will show you new possibilities regarding love and romance.

You will be guided in describing your ideal lover, how to use the Universal Law of Attraction and how to recognize this person when he/she shows up.

You will learn how to open yourself up to all aspects of inviting love and romance into your life.

If you are in an existing relationship, this book will give you a different outlook, provide you with ways to re-energize your relationship, and how to make love and romance fun again. Includes many ideas to re-kindle the flames!

This book will show you how to prepare yourself physically, mentally, and spiritually to attract the ideal person into your life or how to put back the love and romance into an existing relationship. Step out of your comfort zone and try something new!

ISBN-13: 978-1549892738 (Softcover)
ASIN: B076HK1XBK (eBook)

For more information, resources and opportunities that will support your experience of these books, please visit: estellereder.wix.com/publishedbooks

The End.

Made in the USA
Monee, IL
25 April 2021

66794456R00073